I0815271

BECOME A CONSTRUCTION TECHNICIAN

Carpentry, Plumbing & More

Ashley Kuehl

An imprint of Abdo Publishing
abdobooks.com

ABDOBOOKS.COM

Published by Abdo Publishing, a division of ABDO, PO Box 398166, Minneapolis, Minnesota 55439.

Printed in the United States of America, North Mankato, Minnesota
102024
012025

Design: Denise Hamernik, Mighty Media, Inc.
Production: Mighty Media, Inc.
Editor: Katherine Chu

Cover Photographs: Adobe Stock (wood, wrenches); Shutterstock Images (construction background, gas detector, gloves, hammer, hard hat, measuring tape, multimeter, paint roller brush and tray, pencil, saw, tape)

Interior Photographs: Adobe Stock, pp. 10 (middle left), 11 (bottom right), 13 (top middle, middle right, bottom right), 44 (left); Library of Congress, p. 7; Mighty Media, Inc. (project photos), pp. 50, 51; Shutterstock Images, pp. 3, 4, 5 (all), 6 (all), 9, 10 (top left, top middle, top right, bottom left, bottom right), 11 (top left, top middle, top right, middle right, bottom left), 12 (all), 13 (top left, top right, bottom left), 14, 15 (all), 16 (all), 17 (all), 18, 19, 20, 21 (all), 22 (all), 23, 24, 25 (all), 26 (all), 27, 28, 29 (all), 30 (all), 31, 32 (all), 33 (all), 34, 35, 36 (all), 37 (all), 38, 39, 40, 41 (all), 42 (all), 43 (all), 44 (right), 44–45 (background), 46 (all), 47 (all), 48 (all), 48–49 (background), 50–51 (background), 52, 53, 54, 55, 56, 57, 58 (all), 59, 60, 61 (all); The Ironbridge Gorge Museum Trust/Wikimedia Commons, p. 8

Design Elements: Adobe Stock (metal sheet texture, Polaroid frame, sticky notes, tacks, wooden panel texture); Shutterstock Images (blueprint texture)

Library of Congress Control Number: 2024938314

PUBLISHER'S CATALOGING-IN-PUBLICATION DATA

Names: Kuehl, Ashley, author.
Title: Become a construction technician: carpentry, plumbing & more / by Ashley Kuehl
Other Title: carpentry, plumbing & more
Description: Minneapolis, Minnesota : ABDO Publishing, 2025 | Series: Talent to trade | Includes online resources and index.
Identifiers: ISBN 9781098294953 (lib. bdg.) | ISBN 9798384915003 (ebook)
Subjects: LCSH: Carpentry--Juvenile literature. | Plumbing--Juvenile literature. | Construction--Juvenile literature. | Building--Juvenile literature. | Jobs--Juvenile literature. | Trades--Juvenile literature.
Classification: DDC 684.0--dc23

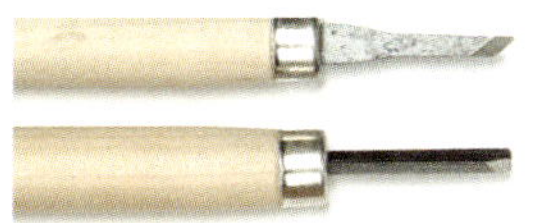

CONTENTS

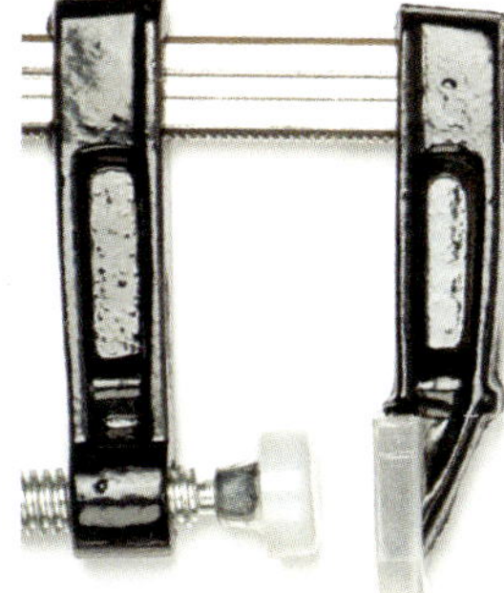

TALENT TO TRADE

Are you captivated by the design of beautiful buildings? Do you love to analyze and solve tricky problems? Do you spend hours making things or taking things apart? Can you imagine yourself leading a team to plan and assemble all the parts and systems of a building? If you answered yes to any of these questions, you might have a future in the construction industry.

Working in construction requires hard physical labor and on-the-job training. But if you enjoy building things or figuring out how they work, you might find the job fun and satisfying.

People working in construction assemble and maintain most of the buildings we use every day. These include schools, homes, shopping centers, factories, and more. Some construction professionals also install and fix complex electrical, heating, and water systems.

In this book, you'll learn about the history of construction. You'll become familiar with some of the key tools, techniques, and skills construction professionals use. You'll find inspiration to start your own career in construction. And finally, you'll learn ways to turn your talents into a trade.

Archaeologists believe ancient humans took about 1,500 years to construct the famous Stonehenge in England. They think construction started around 3000 BCE, with the last change made around 1500 BCE.

The tallest pyramid is the Great Pyramid at Giza. It is about 450 feet (137 m) tall!

HISTORY OF CONSTRUCTION

Humans have assembled structures since before recorded history. In fact, historians named many time periods in human history after the types of tools they used. During the Stone Age, for instance, people made and used stone tools. Around 5500 BCE, people in what is now Serbia started smelting, or adding heat, to copper to make tools. Over the next few centuries, people started using other metals, kicking off the Bronze Age and the Iron Age. Tools, such as metal axes and saws, made it easier to build with wood.

Early in the Bronze Age, humans started making dried bricks out of mud. They put these bricks together with wood and wet mud, building stronger structures. People skilled in creating stone and brick buildings became known as masons. Starting around 4000 BCE, Mesopotamians built big palaces and temples from brick. These structures are some of the earliest historical examples of masonry.

Around 2780 BCE, Egyptians started to build pyramids using heavy stone and lots of human power. Historians still don't know exactly how they moved or cut the stone. The method of building with stone spread. Soon, stone buildings started appearing in Greece and Italy.

Clay also became more developed during this time. Masons fired clay to make bricks, terra-cotta, and tile. Around the second century BCE, Romans improved mortar, a substance that "glued" stone or brick together. Then they created an even stronger substance, often considered by historians to be the first concrete.

Italian artist Leonardo da Vinci used physics and math to design machines around 1500 CE. He's considered one of the most important engineers in history.

The medieval era in Europe began around 500 CE. Trained specialists, such as carpenters, roofers, and stonemasons, became more common. These artisans taught others through apprenticeships. Masters were the most experienced workers. They coordinated most building projects. Journeymen were those with some experience, and the newest learners were apprentices. Builders without specialized training were considered unskilled laborers. Their work was physically demanding and paid by the project or the day. Many modern construction fields still use these terms today.

The Industrial Revolution, which lasted from 1760 to 1913, brought a new and easier way to make iron. Engineers and construction workers started building bridges, water systems, and railroads with it. Next came building with steel and mechanized equipment, making it easier and safer to construct bigger buildings. The first skyscraper was built in Chicago in 1885. It was ten stories high!

New steel techniques also led to prefabrication. Traditionally, an entire house is built on-site. But with prefabrication, parts of a house could be prebuilt in a factory, shipped to the site, and easily assembled. This process was

British ironworker Abraham Darby was the first to smelt iron ore. He used a blast furnace (*pictured*) to make iron pots and other iron items.

As of 2024, the tallest human-made structure in the world is the Burj Khalifa in Dubai. It is 2,717 feet (828 m) tall!

much faster and less expensive than traditional methods because it didn't take workers as long to build a house.

In the 1950s, the United States saw a housing boom. This huge need for homes helped the construction industry grow. Since then, construction technicians, or techs, have developed new building techniques, styles, and materials. Modern construction has also seen a push toward sustainability, or creating buildings and materials that don't harm the environment. Heating and cooling systems use fewer fossil fuels, and plumbing systems use less water.

In the following pages, you'll learn what it takes to work as a professional in the construction industry. You may even be inspired to start your own journey to becoming a construction technician!

TOOLS OF THE TRADE

Get familiar with some of the tools construction professionals use to plan, assemble, and fix buildings and systems.

PREPARATION

BLUEPRINTS

Blueprints are drawn-out or computer-generated guides showing the layout and details of a building and its systems. They are often made to scale. For example, 12 inches (30.5 cm) of space might be represented by 1 inch (2.5 cm) in the blueprint. Most construction professionals use blueprints to figure out measurements of space and materials.

SAFETY EQUIPMENT

Construction techs wear hard hats and safety glasses made of durable plastic to protect them from falling or flying debris. Dust masks and respirators cover and create a seal over a worker's mouth and nose. They filter out dust particles, which can cause lung damage. Workers wear hearing protection, such as earmuffs or earplugs. These prevent hearing damage from noisy power tools or jackhammers. Insulated clothes and accessories protect workers from electrical surges and the cold. This can include gloves made from many layers of rubber and jackets with a thick layer of down, fleece, or synthetic materials.

TAKING APART & PUTTING TOGETHER

CIRCULAR SAWS

A circular saw has a jagged-edged circular blade that cuts wood in a straight line or at an angle. These electric saws are corded or battery-powered. They also include settings that allow them to only cut partway into the wood. Some circular saws have a stronger blade that can cut harder materials, such as metal.

HAMMERS & SCREWDRIVERS

A hammer and nails are used to attach materials. Some hammers have two pieces of metal that come together on one side to pull out a nail. Screwdrivers attach screws to a material. Screws have a threaded surface that helps hold them in place. Because of this, they are better at holding materials together than nails.

PLIERS & WRENCHES

Construction techs use a wide variety of pliers and wrenches depending on the task they are trying to complete. For example, diagonal cutting pliers can be used to cut wires. They can also be used to cut or remove different fasteners, such as pins or nails. And long-nose pliers can reach into small, tight spaces to grab wires or small fasteners, such as staples. Most wrenches can be used to hold, turn, fasten, loosen, or tighten different-sized nuts and bolts. Pipe wrenches can be used on pipes. These are similar to standard wrenches, but usually have teeth that can grip the pipe's smooth surface.

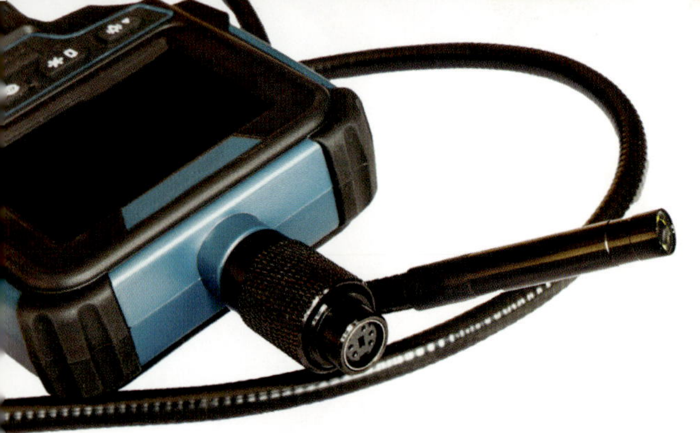

GATHERING INFORMATION

CAMERAS

Construction techs may use special cameras to view spaces they can't fit into. Plumbers use a sewer scope to look inside long pipes. This device has a cable with a camera and lights on one end and a screen on the opposite end. Plumbers may use sewer scopes to find holes or cracks.

Plumbers and electricians may use a thermal or infrared camera to detect temperature and heat differences. Plumbers use this tool to find potential water leaks behind walls. An area with more water will be a different temperature than the surrounding area. Electricians use this tool to find hot or cold spots in electrical equipment.

FINDING ELECTRICITY

An electrician might use a multimeter or voltage tester to figure out why an outlet or switch isn't working. A multimeter plugs into a power source. It measures how much electricity is flowing and if something is slowing it down. A voltage tester can be held next to an outlet or light switch. It can detect whether electricity is flowing or not.

LEAK DETECTORS

A heating, ventilation, and air-conditioning (HVAC) tech might use a leak detector to check for air safety. Leak detectors use thermal imaging to find gases, such as natural gas or carbon monoxide, that can't be detected by feel or smell but can cause health problems. If the HVAC tech finds a gas leak, then they have a better idea of which pipes may need fixing.

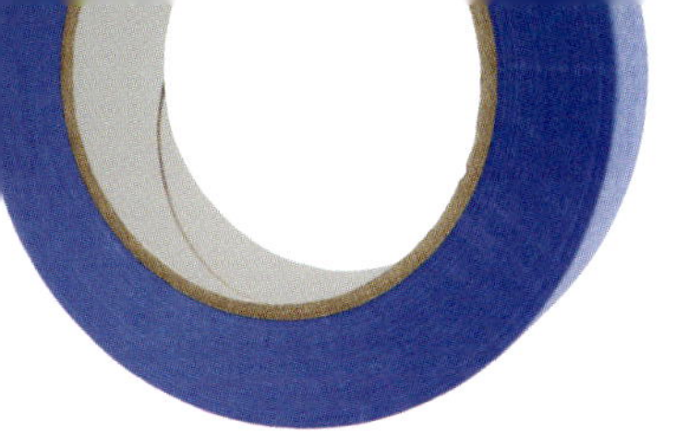

PAINTING

PAINTER'S TAPE

Painter's tape is a wide tape that can be easily pulled off a surface and doesn't leave sticky residue. Painters attach it along corners between walls, ceilings, windowsills, and floors to keep paint off surfaces not meant to be painted. It also helps create sharp, clean edges.

PROTECTION & CLEANING

Painters use canvas drop cloths or plastic tarps to cover floors and furniture. Paint may land on them but won't leak through. Smaller, softer cloths and rags can also help wipe up any spilled paint. Sometimes painters use solvents to clean up spills. Solvents are chemical substances that can dissolve paint. This makes it easy to wipe paint off hard surfaces.

BRUSHES & TRAYS

Painters may use brushes, rollers, or sprayers to apply paint to a surface. Paintbrushes are usually used on edges or smaller areas. Rollers paint large, flat surfaces, such as walls or ceilings. Rollers look like a rolling pin covered with wool-like cloth with a handle connected to one side. They spread paint more evenly than brushes. Painters might also use a paint sprayer to apply large amounts of paint quickly across a larger surface. Most sprayers have a container to hold the paint and a nozzle that sprays paint onto a surface.

Painters might use buckets or paint trays to hold paint. The trays are rectangular containers that have a ridged, angled bottom with a deep space on one end to hold the paint. A painter dips a brush or roller into the paint. Then they use the ridged slope to scrape off any extra, leaving an even coat of paint on the brush or roller.

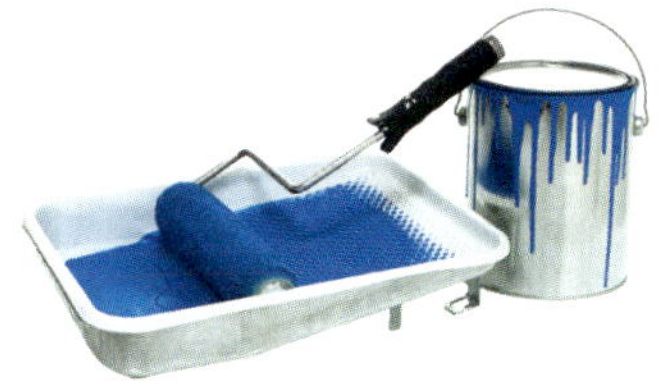

SPECIAL SKILLS

Explore some of the skills that construction technicians need to do their jobs.

COMMUNICATION

Nearly anyone working in the construction industry must listen to and interact with other people. Construction managers explain project details to clients and employees. These can include schedules, budgets, expectations, and more. Laborers need to get along with others and work as part of a team. All construction professionals need to follow plan instructions to complete their tasks.

COORDINATION & ATTENTION TO DETAIL

It's important for construction techs to have good hand-eye coordination as they cut, organize, and put together materials and projects. They also need a good eye for spotting problems or flaws in their projects. Plus, they need to have the ability to rework something that isn't right.

MATH & DRAWING

Almost all construction techs must be able to create and read blueprints and plans. They need to measure materials and available space. Managers need to know the amount of supplies each project needs. Most construction professionals need to estimate the total cost and time needed to complete a project. To do this, math and drawing skills are key.

PROBLEM-SOLVING & PATIENCE

Plumbers, electricians, and HVAC techs look at systems that aren't working. They need to be able to run different tests to figure out what's wrong. An issue in a system might have many complex causes. These workers need to problem-solve and try various solutions to fix any issues.

RESPECT FOR SAFETY

Anyone working with power tools, heavy materials, and equipment must pay attention to safety. They'll need to use safety equipment and understand how to use all of their tools. They must follow the rules and regulations of their trade to make sure buildings and systems are safely constructed and installed.

CAREERS IN CONSTRUCTION

Most construction professionals have a role in assembling or maintaining buildings or other structures. Within the industry, these professionals can specialize in a variety of areas.

CARPENTER

A carpenter builds and fixes objects made of wood and other materials. They may set up scaffolding. This is a temporary structure made of wood planks and metal poles. Scaffolding is set up on the outside of buildings for laborers or other specialists. They use scaffolding when building, fixing, cleaning, or painting a building.

Carpenters also put together the frames of buildings, such as houses, schools, or offices. The frame provides the building with support and shape. Other carpenters specialize in installing drywall, creating furniture, and building cabinets. Some can also install or fix fences, decks, and other structures.

CLIENT CONSULTATION & PLANNING

Most carpentry projects start with a consultation. A client may hire a carpenter to make them a piece of furniture. An architect may hire a carpenter to build a house. Some clients hire carpenters to help with commercial projects, such as constructing a building. After agreeing to a project, carpenters study any blueprints the client provides and make a building plan. This includes the steps for building the project.

MATERIALS

Carpenters may use different materials depending on what they are working on. These include wood, fiberglass, plastic, and drywall. A good carpenter knows about different types of materials and what will work best for each project. For example, some woods are softer or more durable than others. Carpenters also need to work within a client's budget. If a material is difficult to find, it will be more expensive.

MEASURING & CUTTING

Preparing materials for building means lots of measuring. So, carpenters usually have strong geometry skills. Every piece of a building must be the right size and put together at the correct angles. Sloppy edges and corners can look bad. But more importantly, wobbly structures can be dangerous. Once a carpenter has measured everything at least twice, they cut materials to the right sizes and shapes using saws, drills, and other tools.

The client and carpenter may discuss details over multiple meetings. These details can include the materials, budget, schedule, and more.

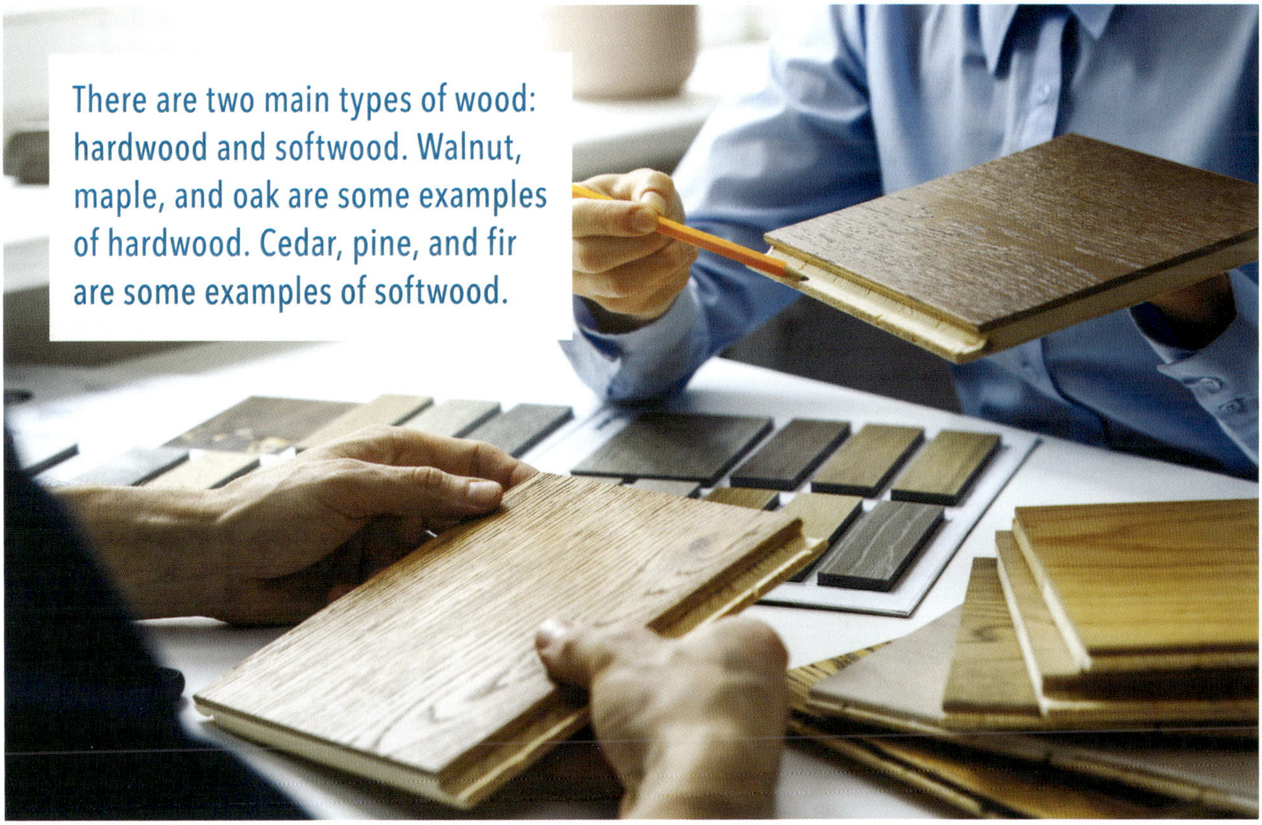

There are two main types of wood: hardwood and softwood. Walnut, maple, and oak are some examples of hardwood. Cedar, pine, and fir are some examples of softwood.

Since many carpenters work on the frames of buildings, it's important they don't have a fear of heights!

Carpenters can use different types of finishes. These include stains, topcoats, and clear finishes.

ASSEMBLY

Carpenters put materials together according to the blueprints. Nails, screws, staples, and glue are used to hold pieces of wood together. A carpenter takes things slowly to avoid mistakes. Mistakes in cutting and assembling materials can be costly. For example, if they cut a piece too short, they may need to buy more. If the carpenter is working on a project run by an architect, the architect may visit the worksite during this phase. They do this to make sure the carpenter is following the original plans.

CHECK, TEST & FINISH

All carpenters measure and test their final product. This includes making sure it's level and sturdy. They may make changes to fix any unevenness. Materials such as wood may need further finishing. Depending on what they are building, carpenters may use a sanding tool to smooth out the surface and apply a finish. Finishes protect the wood and can add or highlight wood color.

CONSTRUCTION MANAGER & LABORER

Construction managers and laborers build and remodel buildings. These include houses, apartment buildings, factories, schools, and office buildings. Construction managers guide a team of laborers, or construction workers. Laborers prepare sites and physically construct buildings or structures.

ESTIMATING COSTS & TIMING

Construction managers set up and lead a construction or remodeling project. They work on many types of projects for a variety of clients. These may include completing a kitchen remodel or building a new factory or apartment complex. Managers may also work with an architect who designs the building.

Managers first meet with clients to understand what they're looking for. Then they create a proposal, which includes a work schedule and a list of supplies and materials. They also figure out how many workers are needed to complete the project. This information is used to estimate the project's budget and how long it will take.

WORKERS & PERMITS

The construction manager orders materials, provides necessary equipment, and hires laborers or other specialists to complete the job. Projects must meet local safety rules and zoning laws. These define what kinds of buildings can be in certain places. Many building projects also require permits from the city or town. Usually, the property owner applies for the permit, but sometimes a contractor can complete the application. This application includes information about what will be built, the materials to be used, and the estimated cost.

Construction managers are also known as general contractors or project managers.

Building permits have different requirements depending on the county and city or town where the structure is being built.

Because heavy machinery can be expensive to buy, many construction managers rent the equipment they need for the duration of the project.

Inspectors take notes and give feedback following each inspection.

PREPARATION

After being hired for a job, laborers prepare the site. They may do this by clearing out debris, digging holes, filling in holes, or compacting loose dirt. Laborers also bring in tools, materials, and equipment. They may put up scaffolding if needed. To help them, laborers use handheld tools and heavy machinery. They may use bulldozers to clear the site and prepare the ground. And they might use a forklift to move or lift heavy materials, such as lumber or concrete.

BUILDING

After the site preparation is complete, the construction manager assigns tasks to the laborers. In a remodel, laborers remove old materials before building or attaching anything new. For both remodels and new builds, laborers may install insulation, a material used inside the exterior walls of a building. It lessens heat loss or gain by creating a barrier between the inside of a building and the outdoors. They may also install siding, a protective material used on the outside of a building. And they may install drywall, a material that makes up the interior walls and ceilings. They also install windows, roofs, and rain gutters.

INSPECTION

Inspectors visit building sites at the beginning of a project and during the construction process. They check that everything matches the permit application and meets local safety and zoning rules. Once the work is complete, the finished project goes through one last thorough inspection.

ELECTRICIAN

Electricians install and maintain electrical systems. They may also work on communications systems and lighting. Clients may hire an electrician to add an electrical system to a newly constructed building. Or an electrician may be hired to fix an existing system that isn't working.

PREPARATION

Before installing a new electrical system, an electrician studies the building plans and blueprints. This shows them where the circuits, outlets, and other electrical equipment are located. It also helps them decide what kind of materials and supplies are needed. Electricians choose different wire types and sizes based on the system's circuit design and how much electricity is needed. Electricians also choose circuit breakers. These provide protection for the electricity flowing within a building's electrical circuit. They may also work with clients to pick out outlets, switches, light fixtures, and more.

INSTALLATION

Electricians usually place wires in the floors, walls, or ceilings. They sometimes need to drill holes to feed wires through. Electrical wires are color coded to show their roles. This helps electricians know which type of wires they are working with. Electricians attach wires from the main electrical panel where the power comes into the building to breaker boxes. The breaker boxes help control the flow of electricity in the building. Sometimes electricians staple wires to boards inside walls or ceilings to keep them in place. If there's a risk of the wires getting bumped or wet, the electrician might run them through protective pipes or tubes.

When installing electrical systems, electricians must follow the National Electrical Code. This is a set of guidelines that ensures electrical systems are installed safely.

When a new building is being constructed, an electrician usually installs the electrical system before the walls or ceilings are installed. This way, they don't need to drill holes.

Because many electrical wires are color coded, electricians need to pass a color-blindness test.

Electricians may place caps on cut wires when installing or fixing outlets. This helps prevent electrical shocks.

TROUBLESHOOTING

If an established electrical system isn't working, an electrician may use a multimeter or a voltage tester to help them find the problem. They can then decide what types of solutions they want to implement to try and fix the issue. Before fixing anything, electricians usually turn the power off at the electrical panel to avoid electrical shocks. Then they use a flashlight or headlamp to see while working.

FIXING WIRES

If wires are broken or not attached properly, electricity can't flow through them. To replace a wire, an electrician cuts a new one using cutting pliers. This tool is strong enough to slice through the wire and its insulation. The electrician will strip the wire ends with a wire stripper. This tool cuts and scrapes the insulation layer off the wire without cutting the wire itself. Electricians also use needle-nose pliers to bend the wire ends. They do this before attaching the ends to other wires or the metal pieces of a light switch or outlet.

PLUMBER

Plumbers build and maintain pipe systems. While some of these pipes transport water, others carry gas, waste, or drainage. Some plumbers may also work on the pipes for heating and cooling systems.

CLEAN WATER & WASTEWATER

A plumber reviews a building's plans and blueprints before installing any plumbing systems. They see where fixtures or appliances such as toilets or dishwashers are supposed to go. Then they plan out where they will put all the pipes. Most buildings have two main types of pipes. One is for clean water and one is for wastewater. In the United States, all clean water that enters a building is safe to drink. This water comes out of faucets and showers and refills recently flushed toilets. Wastewater is the water that drains out after a shower or a toilet flush. It flows to a public water facility for cleaning and sanitizing. It's important that plumbers don't get these pipes mixed up!

PREPARING PIPE

After making their plans, plumbers decide what kinds of pipe they need. Some pipes, such as PEX or copper, can be used for hot and cold water in a home. PEX pipes are often color coded blue and red for cold and hot water. Other kinds of pipes, such as corrugated stainless steel or black steel pipes, are better for gas lines. Plumbers then measure and cut pipes to the right size. Then they prepare pipes for attachment. Plumbers may use a tool called a pipe threader, which trims and shapes the ends of pipes to help them fit together, forming a tight, leakproof seal. Plumbers might also glue or solder pipes together.

Plumbers may help create blueprints to make sure the plumbing system follows building codes. Blueprints also help them decide the amount of materials they need while staying within the project's budget.

Plumbers usually use copper, steel, or plastic pipes for home plumbing systems.

Installing a plumbing system for a new building can take several weeks to several months.

PLACING PIPE

In a new building, the plumbing system may be installed before walls or floors are put in place. Walls and floors are then installed over the pipes. If the walls or floors are already in place, plumbers may need to cut holes to insert pipes. In some buildings, a plumber may attach pipes to the ceiling.

FIXING LEAKS, HOLES & CLOGS

Plumbers fix and replace old or broken pipes and faucets. They may also work on other appliances that use water, such as dishwashers and washing machines. First, they look for leaks or holes. They may decide to patch these with tape, special putty, or other material. They may even replace a pipe with new pieces of pipe.

Plumbers will also fix clogs. They can do this with chemicals to dissolve the clog or a drain snake or auger to pull out a clog. A drain snake has a long cable with a spring or auger on one end and a handle on the other. They are usually used on smaller pipes inside a building. A drain auger is similar to a snake but is larger. Drain augers can be used to unclog larger pipes both inside and outside a building. This can include any pipes that run below a building to a sewer. Plumbers insert the snake or auger tube down a drain to pull out a clog.

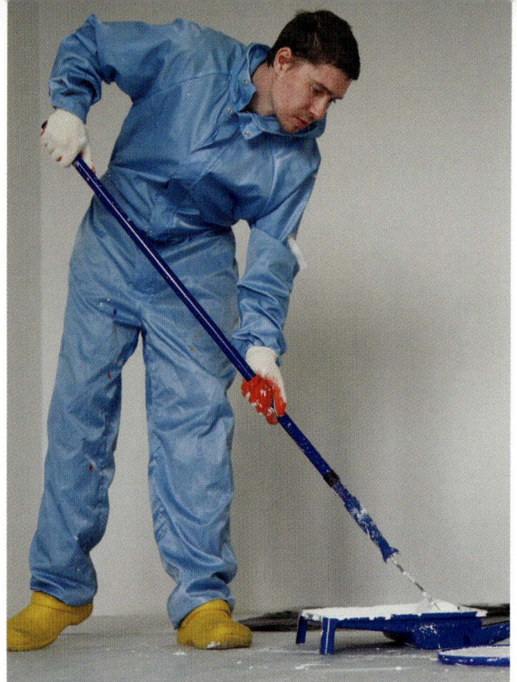

PAINTER

There are different types of painters. Commercial painters work on big buildings, such as office or business buildings. Residential painters work on the interior and exterior parts of a home or other residential building. And industrial painters paint machines and structures, such as equipment, vehicles, bridges, and more.

REMOVING OLD PAINT

When repainting the outside of a building or structure, painters may first remove old paint or dirt with a pressure washer. Pressure washers spray water about 20 times faster than a fire hose. Painters might also apply chemicals called paint strippers to soften and loosen old paint. Then they use a sharp-edged tool called a paint scraper to remove the paint.

SURFACE PREPARATION

Painters use spackle or caulk to fill in any holes or cracks in the walls. These substances are soft when applied and harden as they dry. Painters may also remove or tape off any outlets or switch covers. They might smooth down rough areas using sandpaper or sanding tools. Then painters use tape, tarps, and drop cloths to cover unpainted surfaces. They may also set up ladders to reach high spots.

PAINTING

Painters usually first apply a layer of paint primer or sealer before painting. This protective layer prepares the surface for paint and helps paint stick to it. A painter usually applies multiple coats of paint to a surface. When they are done, painters may apply a finish that seals in the paint. This protects any outside surfaces from weather, sunlight, and other damage.

To complete larger jobs, professional painters may work as a team.

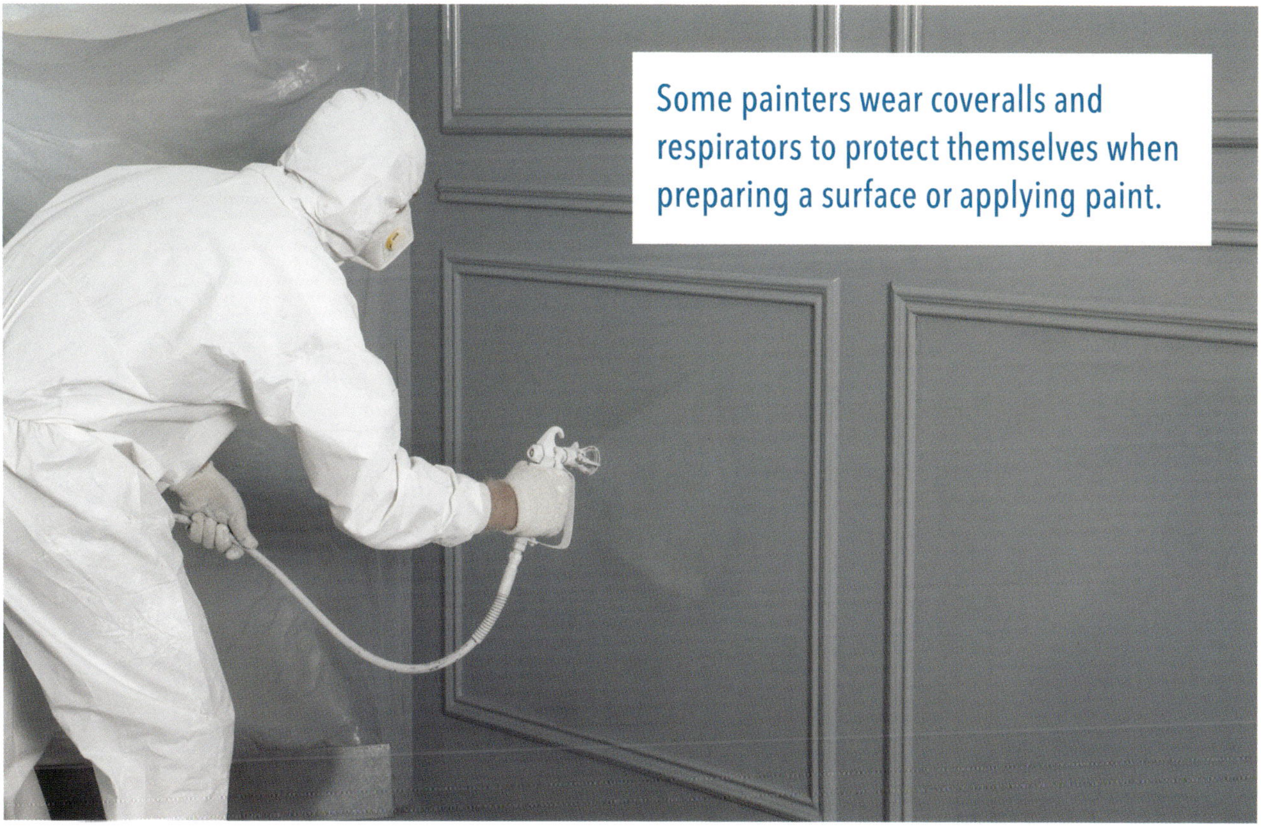

Some painters wear coveralls and respirators to protect themselves when preparing a surface or applying paint.

Technicians may also do some basic electrical wiring for HVAC systems.

HVAC TECHNICIAN

HVAC technicians install, maintain, and repair heating, ventilation, cooling, and refrigeration systems. This includes furnaces, boilers, heat pumps, air-conditioners, and walk-in refrigerators in grocery stores or restaurants. Some techs may focus on one or two of those areas, while others may work on all of them. HVAC techs sometimes work with electricians, plumbers, and other laborers and contractors when completing larger jobs.

INSTALLATION

Before installing a new HVAC system, techs review building plans and blueprints to figure out where to put systems. These include vents, ductwork, or pipes and tubes that carry air in and out. They also need to check every system part to make sure it's doing its job.

INSPECTIONS

Many HVAC systems are complex and should be inspected every year. During an inspection, HVAC techs visually check parts such as ducts, vents, and filters. Techs may use a leak detector to check if pipes or tubes have holes or leaks.

Most heating systems use either furnaces or boilers, which may burn gas to create heat. HVAC techs measure the gas coming in and how efficiently it is burned. They also use a manometer to measure gas pressure. The pressure needs to be in a certain range for the system to work safely.

Techs also inspect ventilation systems, which control the airflow throughout a building. These systems often work together with a heating and cooling system. Part of a tech's job is making sure air circulates safely and that the tubes and pipes that transport gas, called fuel lines, don't have holes. Techs use an anemometer to see how fast air is moving. To check gas levels, they use radon and carbon monoxide detectors. Techs also check air filters, which collect air pollutants.

TESTING & REPAIR

If an HVAC system isn't working, the tech may check the thermostat. These devices set and control the temperature in a building. Techs make sure electricity is running through the system and connecting wires are in good shape.

HVAC systems include many different components, and any one of them can stop working. HVAC techs use detailed checklists to check each component when looking for a problem. Solutions may include cleaning, repairing, and replacing broken parts or wires. Once they fix an HVAC system, techs may complete a follow-up with their client. This includes explaining the problem, how it was fixed, and what it still needs if a larger repair is required.

Technicians clean, repair, or replace parts, such as motors, fans, blowers, and filters.

Technicians may tell customers how to clean and take care of their systems in the future.

CONSTRUCT YOUR VISION

It's time to get creative! What do you love about construction? Create a vision board that reflects this and inspires you. Let it motivate you to turn your talents into your trade!

Put your vision board where you'll see it on a regular basis, such as in your locker or next to your bed.

If you could build a house, what would it look like?

Display magazine pages, photos, and quotes that reflect your interests in construction!
"We shape our buildings; thereafter, they shape us."
—Winston Churchill

SET YOUR FOUNDATION

You don't have to wait until you're 18 to see whether you have an aptitude for construction work. There are many kits or at-home projects you can do to start working on your skills!

Practice sketching the structures or buildings around you. As you sketch, think about how the structure or building fits together.

Search online or borrow a library book about creating your own Lego buildings, and get started at home.

Try out construction,
engineering, or building kits
aimed at teens or adult
beginners.

BUILD YOUR SKILLS

One way to find out if this field is right for you is to try it out!

Find a local plumbers', electricians', or other construction union. Explore any online resources they offer. Ask if you can interview someone about their job, education, and training.

Sign up for an industrial arts, tech, woodshop, or metal shop class to learn some basic skills in repair and construction.

Learn from digital resources. Most home fix-it or building projects will have an online how-to video.

INVOLVE YOUR COMMUNITY

Find people in your life who can help you grow your talents. And find ways to help those around you. You'll develop your people skills as well as your construction skills.

Offer to help a parent or a friend's parent in exchange for teaching you some basics. You could carry supplies and equipment or even take on some easy repair tasks.

Once your fix-it skills are in good shape, set up a fix-it clinic. People can bring their broken items, and you'll help repair them.

Join a youth program that provides job training from real professionals.

CREATE A BIRD FEEDER

Practice your building skills by making a wooden bird feeder. Hang it in your backyard or front porch and add birdseed to attract birds!

STEPS

1 Measure and mark four 4-inch (10.2-cm) long pieces out of two 12-inch (30.5-cm) long square dowels. Use a handsaw and clamps to cut the square dowels at the marks. These will be used for the bird feeder's frame and cross supports. Set them aside. Set the excess wood aside for a different project.

2 Lay the larger piece of basswood flat on the work surface. This will be the bird feeder's base. Create a frame on top of the base with the square dowels. Lay one cut piece from step 1 on top of the base at a narrow side. Lay two 12-inch (30.5-cm) long square dowels on top of the base down its long sides. Lay a second cut piece from step 1 on top of the base to finish the frame.

3 Draw a line on the base where the frame ends. Remove the frame pieces and use the handsaw to cut the base at the mark. Set the excess wood aside for a different project.

4 Put the frame pieces back on top of the base. Use wood glue to secure them in place.

SUPPLIES

- ruler
- pencil
- handsaw
- clamps
- 4 square dowels, ½ by 12 inches (1.3 by 30.5 cm)
- larger basswood board, 4 by 24 inches (10.2 by 61 cm)
- wood glue
- 4 square dowels, ¾ by 4 inches (1.9 by 10.2 cm)
- smaller basswood board, 3 by 24 inches (7.6 by 61 cm)
- hammer
- nails
- 4 eyelet screws
- wide craft sticks (optional)
- glue gun (optional)
- wooden skewers (optional)
- string

5 Make a mark 1 inch (2.5 cm) from the end on one side of each ¾ by 4 inch (1.9 by 10.2 cm) square dowel. Draw a line from the opposite corner to the mark. Saw straight down along the line to create angled pillars.

6 Glue the pillars' flat bottoms to the inside corners of the frame.

7 Nail one cut piece from step 1 between two pillars as a cross support on one narrow side. Repeat on the other side.

8 Saw the smaller basswood piece in half so you have two 12-inch (30.5-cm) long pieces for the bird feeder's roof.

9 Attach the roof pieces to the pillars with wood glue. Hammer a nail through the roof and into each pillar.

10 Hammer an eyelet screw onto each of the four corners of the bird feeder frame. Then screw them in all the way.

11 If you'd like, decorate the bird feeder by cutting craft sticks into shingles and hot gluing them to the roof. You can also cut craft sticks to cover the sides of the roof and add wooden skewers along the edges of the bird feeder.

12 Knot a string to each eyelet screw. Knot the strings together at the top and hang the bird feeder by the knot.

Step 7

Step 11

BECOMING A CONSTRUCTION TECHNICIAN

TRAINING

Do you want to know what it takes to become a construction technician? Education and legal requirements vary by job, but many employers require at least a high school diploma. Some employers may prefer new hires who have technical or community college training. Programs at these schools offer courses in math, physics, and mechanical and electrical systems. Some programs also include classes on budgeting and planning.

Almost all construction jobs are taught through apprenticeships. This means a company will hire someone with little or no experience. Professionals with more experience will train an apprentice while working on real projects for clients.

Apprentices watch and copy the professionals as they do the job. The professionals also make sure apprentices don't make mistakes, follow all regulations, and complete tasks safely and efficiently. Some people may start apprenticeships and school at the same time.

Some states require electricians, plumbers, and HVAC specialists to get a license. This may mean workers have to complete both academic work and on-the-job training. Most attend a college or trade school. Some work as apprentices until they earn their own licenses.

Training requirements for painters vary. Some states require painters to be licensed or certified. Most start by helping a more experienced painter.

FINDING APPRENTICESHIPS

Those who start as an apprentice usually get job offers from the company they trained with. But how do you find an apprenticeship? If you're taking educational courses, talk to teachers and classmates about what you're looking for. Some schools have bulletin boards or online job boards for companies to post job openings. And some programs work with businesses to give students a chance at on-the-job experience.

If you haven't started taking courses, look and apply for apprenticeship programs in your chosen industry. Some programs may require applicants to pass an entrance exam as part of the application process.

FINDING A JOB

Ready for a new role? Register with your state and obtain a license if needed. Different states have different license requirements. Make sure to check your state's requirements for your specialty.

- Before applying for a new position, create a résumé detailing your education and experience. It can include unrelated work that shows you're reliable and willing to learn.

- Keep in contact with teachers and classmates from your program, as well as any managers and coworkers from previous jobs and apprenticeships. Ask them to recommend you if they know people who are hiring. Many get work through people they know, known as network connections.

- Once you get a job, be on time, responsible, and reliable. Listen to your manager and do your best. Every day on the job is a chance to learn something new or improve your skills.

WORKING FOR YOURSELF

After a few years working for someone else, some construction professionals decide to start their own businesses. If you do this, you will still likely need a résumé to showcase the projects you've worked on. You might also consider marketing your services to potential clients. Build a business website that includes a portfolio of work you've done. Post advertisements on public bulletin boards, in local newspapers or magazines, or online. This helps potential clients know who you are and what you can do.

Continue to network with others in your industry. A good reference or testimonial can go a long way. If a potential client trusts someone who recommends you, they're likely to trust you too.

KEEP GOING

Having a job doesn't mean you stop learning. Construction work is varied. As you do more jobs, you'll learn new and different techniques. As you gain experience, you may also gain responsibility. That could include being promoted to supervising roles or completing more difficult or specialized tasks.

Rules and guidelines may also change over time. Staying updated on safety rules is important for all construction techs. These might include new kinds of materials, tools, and local safety and zoning codes. If you need a license, be sure to renew it as needed.

You might choose to specialize in a particular area. Or you might find you like a different role better than what you trained for. Learning and moving around is always an option. You can continue to take courses to learn more in your field or get a higher-level job.

To advance and become a master, carpenters need to get a certification. Master electricians need to meet certain requirements and have work experience. And master plumbers must pass a test and have work experience.

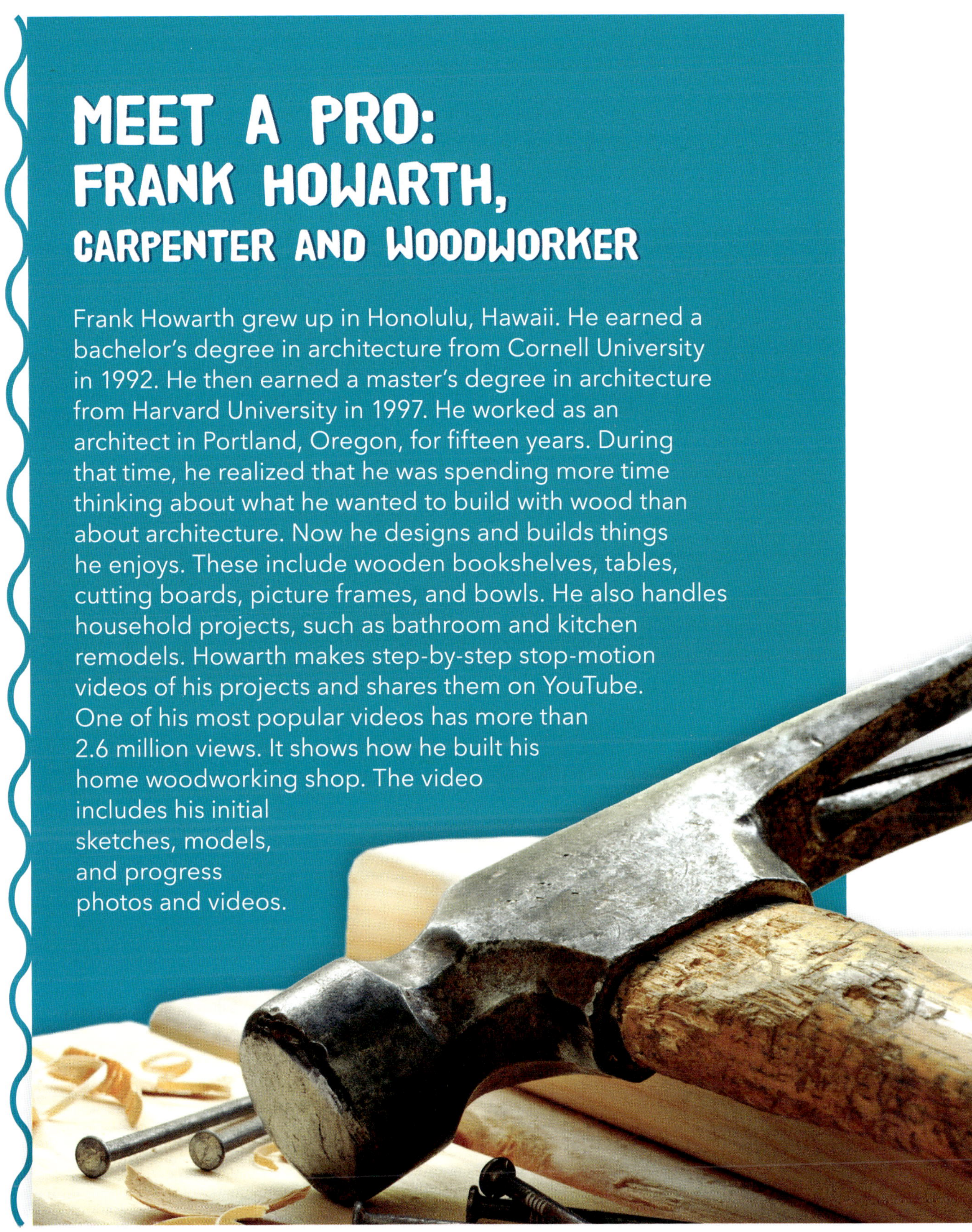

MEET A PRO: FRANK HOWARTH, CARPENTER AND WOODWORKER

Frank Howarth grew up in Honolulu, Hawaii. He earned a bachelor's degree in architecture from Cornell University in 1992. He then earned a master's degree in architecture from Harvard University in 1997. He worked as an architect in Portland, Oregon, for fifteen years. During that time, he realized that he was spending more time thinking about what he wanted to build with wood than about architecture. Now he designs and builds things he enjoys. These include wooden bookshelves, tables, cutting boards, picture frames, and bowls. He also handles household projects, such as bathroom and kitchen remodels. Howarth makes step-by-step stop-motion videos of his projects and shares them on YouTube. One of his most popular videos has more than 2.6 million views. It shows how he built his home woodworking shop. The video includes his initial sketches, models, and progress photos and videos.

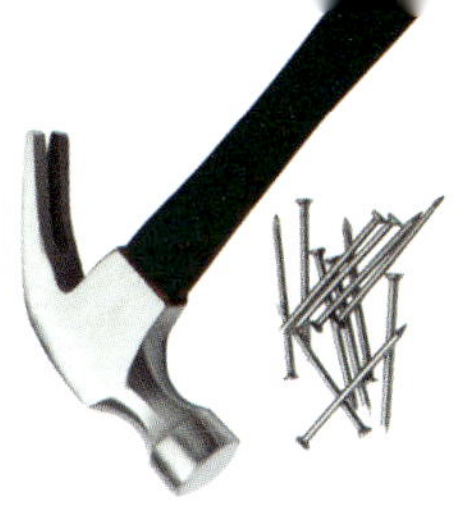

TRADES AT WORK

EARNING POTENTIAL

The US Bureau of Labor Statistics provides estimated wage ranges for most workers in any given job category. The average salaries below are from May 2023. While these estimates provide a sense of what you could expect to earn, actual salaries can vary greatly depending on where you work, your level of experience, and any specialized skills you have.

GROW YOUR POTENTIAL

Whatever salary you start at, there are various ways to grow your earning potential throughout your career. Here are a few ways to boost your income while continuing to do what you love.

Find a specialty. Within most construction fields, techs can specialize in one area. A plumber might specialize in ceiling fire sprinklers, which turn on automatically if there's a fire.

A carpenter might specialize in unique and detailed carvings on furniture or doorway trim. Becoming an expert means you can charge more for your services.

JOB CATEGORY	ANNUAL SALARY
Carpenters	$46,000-$72,000
Construction Managers	$82,000-$136,000
Construction Laborers	$37,000-$57,000
Electricians	$48,000-$80,000
Plumbers	$48,000-$80,000
Painters	$39,000-$59,000
HVAC Mechanics and Installers	$47,000-$71,000

Become your own boss. Once you are an experienced construction tech, you might choose to start your own business. You'd be responsible for finding new projects and negotiating with clients. You might hire laborers or techs for specific jobs. Or you might grow your business and hire full-time employees. Those that own successful companies are strong leaders that are comfortable with making big decisions. They also need to be good with money and numbers. And they are excellent at communicating with both clients and workers.

Train new techs. As you gain experience in your field, you'll likely start training new apprentices. In addition to that, you might choose to teach courses at your local community college or trade school. An experienced tech can come up with new curriculum for learners.

FINANCIAL SMARTS

However you make money, it's important to manage your finances wisely.

If you have an employer, you will receive a regular paycheck from them. This income will be your wages minus taxes. If your

employer offers health insurance, retirement savings, or any other benefits, those will also be deducted from your take-home pay. Financial experts recommend you put about 20 percent of each paycheck into savings and try to keep an emergency fund with enough money to cover three to six months' worth of living expenses.

If you are self-employed, you will receive payments directly from your clients. You'll need to track this income along with your business expenses, such as tools and materials. Self-employed individuals must also pay their own taxes, generally four times a year, since they don't have an employer withholding taxes from each paycheck. Business owners use the remaining profits to pay themselves as well as fund savings accounts—for both themselves and their businesses!

If you have employees, you must pay both your employees and yourself. You will manage your company's payroll, employee benefits, business insurance, and more. If you are responsible for making client bids and project budgets, you will use all of this information to know how much you'll need to charge a client. This takes a lot of work and organization. But hiring employees can let you take on bigger and more complex jobs. It can also give you more time to focus on working with clients and finding new business.

K1
K2
K3
K4
K6
K10

DO WHAT YOU LOVE!

Working in the construction industry can be hard work. It requires an ability to put things together, an understanding of blueprints and plans, attention to detail, and a willingness to solve tricky problems. You'll also need to be able to learn by watching and doing. If you're good at making and following through with design plans and you're able to stick to a schedule and a budget, you might be good at construction work.

Many people love to design and build structures and fix equipment and systems. You can see your hard work when you pass by a building you worked on or test out a faucet or power outlet that you fixed. Maybe your goal is to be a carpenter who specializes in building furniture. You may want to manage a team that builds houses. Or perhaps you just want to fix the things that break in your home. As long as you find work you love, you'll love what you do.

GLOSSARY

analyze–to examine something to find out what it is or what makes it work.

architecture–the art of planning and designing structures. A person who practices architecture is called an architect.

artisan–a person skilled in a craft or a trade.

auger–a helix-shaped tool or part.

carbon monoxide–a colorless and odorless toxic gas.

component–one of the parts or units of a combination, mixture, or system.

drywall–a board that is made of multiple layers of fiber, paper, or felt bonded to a sheet of plaster.

efficient–in a way that does not waste time or energy.

finish–a final protective coat or treatment for wood.

industrial–of or having to do with factories and making things in large quantities.

Industrial Revolution–a period in England from about 1750 to 1850. It marked the change from an agricultural to an industrial society.

infrared–energy transmitted by waves, which can be felt as heat.

insulation–material that provides a protective layer or coating.

negotiate–to work out an agreement about the terms of something.

network–to join or communicate with a group of people. The group is also called a network.

payroll–the money paid by a company to its employees.

PEX pipe–cross-linked polyethylene pipe. A bendable plastic pipe that comes in blue, red, white, and orange colors.

potential–capable of being or becoming, or something that could be.

radon–a radioactive gas.

residue–what remains after something is taken off.

solder–to unite or repair using a melted mixture of metals.

specialize—to develop expertise in a certain area, called a specialty. A person who does this is a specialist.

synthetic—something that is human-made by a chemical process. Synthetic products include plastic and many kinds of fabrics, dyes, and drugs.

technical—related to special knowledge of how a particular kind of work is done. A technician or tech is someone who is skilled at a task requiring special knowledge. Technique is a way of doing a task using special knowledge or skills.

thermal—relating to heat or changes in temperature.

thermostat—a device that controls temperature, especially in a building.

ventilation—the movement of air through a room or other space.

voltage—electric force measured in volts.

ONLINE RESOURCES

To learn more about trades in construction, please visit **abdobooklinks.com** or scan this QR code. These links are routinely monitored and updated to provide the most current information available.

INDEX